Key Stage 3

Year 9 Workbook

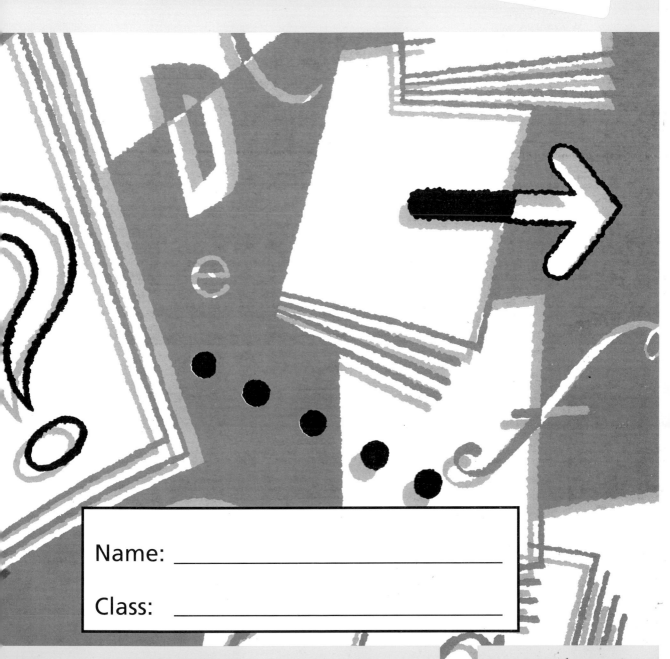

Name: _____

Class: _____

English

Jeff Morton

First published 1999

Letts Educational
9–15 Aldine Street
London W12 8AW
Tel 0181 740 2270
Fax 0181 740 2280

Text: © Jeff Morton 1999

Design and illustrations © BPP (Letts Educational) Ltd 1999

Design and page layout: Ken Vail Graphic Design, Cambridge

Illustrations: Sylvie Poggio Artists Agency (Nick Duffy, Rosalind Hudson, Paul McCaffrey, Phil Smith and Sarah Warburton)

British Library Cataloguing–in–Publication Data

A CIP record for this book is available from the British Library

ISBN 1 84085 217 8

Printed and Bound

Letts Educational is the trading name of
BPP (Letts Educational) Ltd

Acknowledgements
The photograph on p25 reproduced by kind permission of the BBC, © BBC. Text extracts reproduced by kind permission: pp6-9, approximately 1,500 words (pp93-97) from *Roll of Thunder, Hear My Cry* by Mildred D. Taylor (Victor Gollancz/Hamish Hamilton, 1977) copyright © Mildred D. Taylor, 1976; p13, *A Blade of Grass* © Brian Patten, 1981, from the anthology *Love Poems*, first published by George, Allen and Unwin Ltd, reproduced by permission of the author, c/o Rogers, Coleridge & White Ltd; pp22-26 from *The Complete Fawlty Towers* by Connie Booth and John Cleese, published by Methuen Publishing Limited; p47, *Horrible Histories: The Terrible Tudors* by Terry Deary and Neil Young, © Terry Deary and Neil Young, first published by Scholastic Ltd

Contents

Introduction

Units

1	Your life is a story	1
2	A painful lesson	6
3	Love hurts	12
4	The execution	16
5	A touch of class	22
6	*The Cloud Child*	29
7	Mirror, mirror…	35
8	The trouble with parents	39
9	Making history: the truth about Henry VIII	46
10	Travelling and writing	52

Introduction: for teachers

This is one of a series of three books, for Years 7, 8 and 9, which have been compiled to support the teaching programme in the Letts *Classbook* for Key Stage 3 English.

Each of the books is free-standing and has been designed so pupils may use it independently, as a 'workbook'. However, it is likely that this book, and the series, will prove most valuable when used in conjunction with the *Classbook* and with each unit of work introduced through classroom discussion.

The intention of the series is to provide a wider range of texts and writing tasks, that give opportunities to reinforce and extend the knowledge and communication skills established through the *Classbook*. Each book does not cover the same genres – or periods – nor attempt to cover the full range of possible genres, but over the series, teachers should find sufficient variety to enable them, in conjunction with the *Classbook*, to address the requirements of the National Curriculum programmes of study for Key Stage 3 English.

Hence, the focus in these books is on understanding and response, and writing practice. The extracts are supported by questions that encourage learning about genre characteristics. A 'twin-pronged' focus on the texts is suggested: detailed consideration of word/sentence issues, and reflection on broader matters of a whole text/genre nature. Each writing task is genre-specific and designed to reinforce the learning acquired in answering the questions, by encouraging pupils to demonstrate their understanding through practice in their own work.

It is also hoped that, over the whole series and within each book, the texts provide a good range in terms of difficulty and interest to pupils. Each teacher will need to guide pupils towards appropriate material, but the intention is that extracts should be stimulating and challenging. Within the series, the Year 7 book is intended to build a bridge between the methods and habits of working of the National Literacy Strategy at Key Stage 2 and secondary school approaches to English. The Year 8 book links with this and leads pupils towards the strategies of the Year 9 book, which is intended to point pupils forward to the work of their GCSE course at Key Stage 4.

How to use this workbook: for pupils

The format of each unit of this book is quite straightforward. You should read through the text extracts to get an idea of basic meaning and then, working with a partner, in groups, or with your teacher, discuss related issues and topics, as an introduction to the passages' subject matter. Suggested topics for discussion include 'reminders' of key words and concepts you are likely to need in developing your answers to the questions in the 'Closer reading' section. You may attempt the answers on your own, or as part of classwork.

The 'Writing practice' section is self-explanatory. For each unit there is a specific task, which focuses on the sort of writing you have just encountered in the passages you have read and discussed. Guidance is given: to help you select subject matter, to plan the organisation and structure of your writing, and to use appropriate means of expression.

The 'Follow up!' suggestions are intended to be just that – further projects you may wish to work on as an 'optional extra', or that your teacher might want to develop into a larger class project.

This book supports the work you did in the *Classbook*. The process of gradually broadening and strengthening your skills continues here, as a further selection of texts and tasks introduces you to an ever-increasing range of materials and activities.

John Green

In his autobiography, *Is That It?*, Bob Geldof tells the story of how he became an international superstar. In the early 1980s, his band, The Boomtown Rats, sold more records than any other in the UK. Later on he became even more famous as the man who organised Live Aid, the biggest ever charity pop concert. Here he explains how he first became involved in pop music.

Forming a band

Soon after I had got back from Canada, I went down to the pub and met Gary Roberts. He was not a close friend, but I had spent some time with him when I was unemployed after leaving school. He was drinking with Johnny Moylett, the younger brother of my friend Pat from Murray's Record Centre. They were talking about forming a band. Gary was a guitarist and Johnny played the piano.

The talk continued over coffee back in the large kitchen at Gary's house, where the Aga stove stayed warm until the small hours. Johnny's cousin, Pat Cusack, was also talking of starting a band, together with a friend of his called Gerry Cott. We knew Gerry, he used to play blues guitar at parties. Pat, Gerry and Johnny were all studying architecture.

'Why don't you all get together?' I suggested. 'That would give you keyboards and three guitars. One of you could play bass.'

'They want to play blues, or something,' Johnny said.

'Well, you could give it a try,' I said. 'The main thing is not to behave like a local band. It's vital to get your act together from the start. It's no good just doing any old style of thing, a Doors song here, a bit of blues there. You need a clear image right from the start.'

'Yeah.'

'You need to act like stars right from the word go. Even with people who know you, you have to behave as if you're special.'

'Yeah, you're right.'

A couple of days later I asked what progress had been made. None, they said. I was not surprised. I was used to people in Dublin talking late at night in their kitchens.

'Ask Pat and Gerry over on Monday, will you?' I said to Johnny.

That same day Gary saw an ad in the paper and bought an electric guitar. It was the band's first proper instrument. Next day I went into the city with him and he bought a Meazzi 100-watt amp. We were very excited. All afternoon we played with it in his room. It had an echo and it flashed off and on in time with whatever rhythm was being played. His mother told us to shut up.

I had known Gary Roberts dimly for years. He went to a Quaker school in Waterford and I had seen him in the holidays screaming around corners on his Honda. Now he went to Trinity College. He had done a year of psychology and a year of medicine. He wanted to give that up and start something else. He was very clever but easily influenced by others. He was a great guitar player but a poor organiser.

Gary said, 'Perhaps you'd better be our manager and get things organised.'

'Yeah, OK,' I said.

After his mother had told us to be quieter, I was playing harmonica while he played acoustic guitar. We were playing 'The Prodigal Son' from the Rolling Stones' *Beggars' Banquet* album. I was singing.

'Why don't you be the lead singer as well?' he said.

I did not really want to. Anyway, I could not sing.

'Yeah, maybe, I don't know,' I said.

Next day I went down to Johnny's place. Johnny Moylett was the baby-faced brother of Pat. He was quiet. He had gone to school in Limerick, where he took piano lessons. He had been a member of the Beatles' fan club. He was very different from his brother, who was always on the look-out for some new scheme that would make him millions or at least a living. Pat made things happen. Johnny let things happen to him. He was always sleepy, it seemed, in everything but his music. He is very likeable. People do not mind doing things for him. I think he knows that and uses it. Pat and Gerry said they would give it a try. That gave us three guitars and keyboards and a singer. It was enough to start.

One Saturday afternoon, Gary, Johnny, Gerry and I met in Pat Moylett's basement flat. Johnny had bought a Tiger electric pianette. Pat had one or two borrowed drums but was pretty useless at keeping time, so it became clear that we needed to get a drummer quickly. Gary blasted everyone out of it with his Meazzi amp. Gerry tried to play bass on an acoustic guitar.

'OK,' I said. 'What sort of music are we going to do? We have to pick one thing and stick with it.'

'Well, I thought Doobie Brothers sort of thing,' said Gary.

'Oh, that's crap,' I said. 'We can't do that.'

'Why not?'

'It means nothing, that sort of music. It has no passion or excitement. It's not about anything real. It has to be something different. Something that isn't just copying. We need to get back to basics – R & B and dance music – and then make out our own direction from there.'

All of us liked R & B. It was our common sixties heritage and Gerry and Gary could play it. We did not know that there were bands all over Britain and America who were thinking the same thing. People were going into pubs because that was where these new bands were playing. They had feeling and conviction. Established pop music was saying nothing.

Talk about

- What features make autobiographies different from other forms of writing?
- How does Geldof maintain the reader's interest?
- What is a first-person narrator? What difference does this make to the way the story is told?

Closer reading

Word and sentence work

1 If you had to make notes about this extract, you would have to pick out the most important features and explain them in your own words, to make sure you had understood everything.

- In each paragraph, highlight what you think is the most important feature – the key word or phrase.

- List the five you consider essential and write a short sentence to go with each, so that you have five sentences which summarise the whole extract.

2 Look at the style of writing. Geldof uses a lot of devices that make it very conversational, e.g. the way he uses slang and abbreviations.

- Who do you think is the intended audience for his book?

- Pick out features of style and content that prove your point.

3 What do we find out about Bob Geldof's character?

- Which of the following terms do you think might be used to describe him? Choose the three you think are most suitable and link each one with a short quote from the text to prove your point.

assertive	sensible	ambitious
loyal	idealistic	naive
patient	confident	sociable
thoughtful	relaxed	responsible

Text and genre work

4 The extract is a mixture of vital information we need to know to understand the chain of events that lead to Geldof's success, and other information that appears much less important.

- Highlight those parts of the extract you consider unnecessary.

- Why do you think he includes these details?

5 How does Geldof show that he took a leading role from the very beginning of the band's life?

6 List what you consider the four most important steps in forming the band.

7 Like many successful bands, the early days of The Boomtown Rats do not seem very promising. Yet even then, there are indications that this group is different, that it has something special.

- List these features.

8 Pop stars, politicians, TV personalities, sportsmen and women, criminals and industrialists – all sorts of people have had their autobiographies published.

- Why do you think people are so keen to read them?

- Why are people so fascinated by the lives of others?

- Whose autobiography would you most like to read? Why?

Writing practice: write your own autobiography

Most people's lives are made up of routine and trivial incidents, with occasional important events. These events form the backbone of your autobiography. Readers will only be interested in the things in your life that make it different from theirs.

These can be:

- a turning point in your life

- something that has changed the way you think or live

- what you want out of life in future

- the way you relate to the people in your life.

Alternatively, they can be events that have no real significance but stick in your mind because they were funny or unusual. You can include either or both in the piece you write, but remember an autobiography might have a wide audience. You might find it useful to look back at your answer to number 6 on the previous page to give you ideas about the style of writing you want to use. You will need to think about the kind of audience you want to attract.

Write about no more than three incidents. If you include more than this, you may find yourself becoming repetitive. If you don't feel you can remember anything, try looking through old photograph albums – the pictures may inspire you. Think back to the first thing you can remember. It must have stuck in your mind for a reason!

You will need to include:

- enough description of people and places to give the reader a clear picture

- some idea about your thoughts and feelings at the time

- details about why you can remember this event.

Follow up!

Find an autobiography you think you would enjoy, or read through some of the ones written by other members of your class. As you read, ask yourself what the writers include that make it interesting.

Classbook reference
Unit 6,
pages 55–6

For Cassie Logan, growing up in 1930s Mississippi is hard. At eight years old, she doesn't understand the 'rules' which govern relationships between black and white and finding out about them can be painful. In this extract from Mildred Taylor's book *Roll of Thunder, Hear My Cry*, Cassie is paying her first visit to town with her grandmother, whom she calls 'Big Ma'. After selling produce from their farm at the local market, Big Ma needs to visit a lawyer, which leaves Cassie, her brother Stacey and his friend T.J. to pay a visit to the shop, where T.J. needs to buy things for his family

When the woman's order was finally filled, Mr Barnett again picked up T.J.'s list, but before he had gotten the next item his wife called, 'Jim Lee, these folks needing help over here and I got my hands full.' And as if we were not even there, he walked away.

'Where's he going?' I cried.

'He'll be back,' said T.J., wandering away.

After waiting several minutes for his return, Stacey said, 'Come on, Cassie, let's get out of here.' He started toward the door and I followed. But as we passed one of the counters, I spied Mr Barnett wrapping an order of pork chops for a white girl. Adults were one thing; I could almost understand that. They ruled things and there was nothing that could be done about them. But some kid who was no bigger than me was something else again. Certainly Mr Barnett had simply forgotten about T.J.'s order. I decided to remind him and, without saying anything to Stacey, I turned around and marched over to Mr Barnett.

'Uh . . . 'scuse me, Mr Barnett,' I said, as politely as I could, waiting a moment for him to look up from his wrapping. 'I think you forgot, but you was waiting on us 'fore you was waiting on this girl here, and we been waiting a good while now for you to get back.'

The girl gazed at me strangely, but Mr Barnett did not look up. I assumed that he had not heard me. I was near the end of the counter so I nicely went to the other side of it and tugged on his shirt sleeve to get his attention.

He recoiled as if I had struck him.

'Y-you was helping us,' I said, backing to the front of the counter again.

'Well, you just get your little black self back over there and wait some more,' he said in a low, tight voice.

I was hot. I had been as nice as I could be to him and here he was talking like this. 'We been waiting on you for near an hour,' I hissed, 'while you 'round here waiting on everybody else. And it ain't fair. You got no right.'

'Whose little nigger is this?' bellowed Mr Barnett.

know he ain't fair making us wait.'

'She your sister, boy?' Mr Barnett spat across the counter.

Stacey bit his lower lip and gazed into Mr Barnett's eyes. 'Yessir.'

'Then you get her out of here,' he said, with hateful force. 'And make sure she don't come back till yo' mammy teach her what she is.'

'I already know what I am!' I retaliated. 'But I betcha you don't know what you are! And I could sure tell you, too, you ole …'

Stacey jerked me forward, crushing my hand in the effort, and whispered angrily, 'Shut up, Cassie!' His dark eyes flashed malevolently as he pushed me in front of him through the crowd.

As soon as we were outside, I whipped my hand from his. 'What's the matter with you? You know he was wrong!'

Stacey swallowed to flush his anger, then said gruffly, 'I know it and you know it, but he don't know it, and that's where the trouble is. Now come on 'fore you get us into a real mess. I'm going up to Mr Jamison's to see what's keeping Big Ma.'

'What 'bout T.J.?' I called, as he stepped into the street.

Stacey laughed wryly. 'Don't worry 'bout T.J. He knows exactly how to act.' He crossed the street sullenly then, his hands jammed in his pockets.

I watched him go, but did not follow. Instead, I ambled along the

Everyone in the store turned and stared at me. 'I ain't nobody's little nigger!' I screamed, angry and humiliated. 'And you ought not be waiting on everybody 'fore you wait on us.'

'Hush up, child, hush up,' someone whispered behind me. I looked around. A woman who had occupied the wagon next to ours at the market looked down upon me. Mr Barnett, his face red and eyes bulging, immediately pounced on her.

'This gal yourn, Hazel?'

'No, suh,' answered the woman meekly, stepping hastily away to show she had nothing to do with me. As I watched her turn her back on me, Stacey emerged and took my hand.

'Come on, Cassie, let's get out of here.'

'Stacey!' I exclaimed, relieved to see him by my side. 'Tell him! You sidewalk trying to understand why Mr Barnett had acted the way he had. More than once I stopped and gazed over my shoulder at the mercantile. I had a good mind to go back in and find out what had made Mr Barnett so mad. I actually turned once and headed toward the store, then remembering what Mr Barnett had said about my returning, I swung back around, kicking at the sidewalk, my head bowed.

It was then that I bumped into Lillian Jean Simms.

'Why don't you look where you're going?' she asked huffily. Jeremy and her two younger brothers were with her. 'Hey, Cassie,' said Jeremy.

'Hey, Jeremy,' I said solemnly, keeping my eyes on Lillian Jean.

'Well, apologize,' she ordered.

'What?'

'You bumped into me. Now you apologize.'

I did not feel like messing with Lillian Jean. I had other things on my mind. 'Okay,' I said, starting past, 'I'm sorry.'

Lillian Jean sidestepped in front of me. 'That ain't enough. Get down in the road.'

I looked up at her. 'You crazy?'

'You can't watch where you going, get in the road. Maybe that way you won't be bumping into decent white folks with your little nasty self.'

This second insult of the day was almost more than I could bear. Only the thought of Big Ma up in Mr Jamison's office saved Lillian Jean's lip. 'I ain't nasty,' I said, properly holding my temper in check, 'and if you're so afraid of getting bumped, walk down there yourself.'

I started past her again, and again she got in my way. 'Ah, let her pass, Lillian Jean,' said Jeremy. 'She ain't done nothin' to you.'

'She done something to me just standing in front of me.' With that, she reached for my arm and attempted to push me off the sidewalk. I braced myself and swept my arm backward, out of Lillian Jean's reach. But someone caught it from behind, painfully twisting it, and shoved me off the sidewalk into the road. I landed bottom first on the ground.

Mr Simms glared down at me. 'When my gal Lillian Jean says for you to get yo'self off the sidewalk, you get, you hear?'

Behind him were his sons R.W. and Melvin. People from the store began to ring the Simmses, 'Ain't that the same little nigger was cuttin' up back there at Jim Lee's?' someone asked.

'Yeah, she the one,' answered Mr Simms. 'You hear me talkin' to you, gal? You 'pologize to Miz Lillian Jean this minute.'

I stared up at Mr Simms, frightened. Jeremy appeared frightened too. 'I – I apologized already.'

Jeremy seemed relieved that I had

spoken. 'She did, Pa. Right now, 'fore y'all come, she did.'

Mr Simms turned an angry gaze upon his son and Jeremy faltered, looked at me, and hung his head.

Then Mr Simms jumped into the street. I moved away from him, trying to get up. He was a mean-looking man, red in the face and bearded. I was afraid he was going to hit me before I could get to my feet, but he didn't. I scrambled up and ran blindly for the wagon. Someone grabbed me and I fought wildly, attempting to pull loose. 'Stop, Cassie!' Big Ma said. '*Stop*, it's me. We're going home now.'

'Not 'fore she 'pologizes to my gal, y'all ain't,' said Mr Simms. Big Ma gazed down at me, fear in her eyes, then back at the growing crowd. 'She

jus' a child.'

'Tell her, Aunty.'

Big Ma looked at me again, her voice cracking as she spoke.

'Go on, child … apologize.'

'But, Big Ma.'

Her voice hardened. 'Do like I say.' I swallowed hard.

'Go on!'

'I'm sorry,' I mumbled.

'I'm sorry, Miz Lillian Jean,' demanded Mr Simms.

A painful tear slid down my cheek and my lips trembled. 'I'm sorry … M-Miz … Lillian Jean.'

When the words had been spoken, I turned and fled crying into the back of the wagon. No day in all my life had ever been as cruel as this one.

Talk about

- What makes this scene particularly dramatic?

- What are the main differences between the characters? Think about their ages, colour and relationships to each other.

- What is distinctive about the way language is used? Do different characters use language in different ways? Think about how dialect is used.

Closer reading

Word and sentence work

1 Pick out the distinctive features in the way the characters speak. Highlight in different colours those which are explained by accent or pronunciation ('No suh'), those where colloquial or slang words are used ('ain't') and those which depend on grammatical construction ('You crazy?').

2 Each of the main characters shows anger in a number of different ways. Make a list of short quotes, linked to each character, which show these differences, and explain what they tell us about each character's attitude to themselves and others.

3 Mildred Taylor uses carefully selected details to show what is happening and how characters feel, rather than describing everything that happens. For example, in the last part of the extract, instead of describing Cassie's face, the way she stands and the way she speaks, she simply says 'My lips trembled'. Highlight other examples of this kind of careful use of detail. The parts you identify should be short phrases rather than whole sentences.

Text and genre work

4 How does Mildred Taylor make Mr Simms seem a frightening figure?

5 What are the main differences between Lillian Jean and her brother, Jeremy?

6 'No day in all my life had ever been as cruel as this one.' In order of importance, explain the things that make this a difficult day for Cassie.

7 What makes Cassie finally approach Mr Barnett?

8 How is Stacey's and T.J.'s behaviour different from Cassie's? How do you think they feel about the way she is treated? What evidence is there in the passage to support your view?

Writing practice

When she gets home that night, Big Ma writes about the day's events in her diary, including her feelings about all those involved and an explanation of her own actions. Write her diary entry.

You could use the following openings for the first five paragraphs, or you could make up your own structure.

● One day Cassie is going to get us into real trouble…

● I suppose Jim Lee Barnett is nothing but a bully, at least that's how Cassie sees it. But white folks think…

● The worst thing was when Lillian Jean started…

● I know Cassie blamed me for the way I handled things. She doesn't understand that I had to…

● Cassie's strong. She'll get over today, given time, but for now we've got to…

Follow up!

Mildred Taylor's book has a sequel, called *Let the Circle be Unbroken*. Try reading both books. For a slightly different way of looking at relationships between black and white people in America, try *To Kill a Mockingbird* by Harper Lee.

Classbook reference
Unit 13,
pages 131–5

It's not surprising that there are a lot of differences between the poems in this unit, since one was written in the sixteenth century and the other is a twentieth-century piece. There are also important similarities, however: they are both love poems and are both about the pain love can cause.

- Read through the poems quickly. Jot down your first reactions to them and what you think are the most obvious differences between them.

A sonnet is a poem which is 14 lines long. It has ten syllables on each line and usually has a strong rhyming pattern.

Sonnet

I find no peace and all my war is done.
I fear and hope, I burn and freeze like ice,
I fly above the wind yet can I not arise.
And naught I have and all the world I seize on.
That looseth nor locketh holdeth me in prison
And holdeth me not, yet can I scape no wise,
Nor letteth me live nor die at my device
And yet of death it giveth me occasion.
Without eyes I see and without tongue I plain.
I desire to perish and yet I ask health.
I love another and thus I hate myself.
I feed me in sorrow and laugh in all my pain.
Likewise displeaseth me both death and life,
And my delight is causer of this strife.

Sir Thomas Wyatt

A Blade of Grass

You ask for a poem
I offer you a blade of grass
You say it is not good enough
You ask for a poem.

I say this blade of grass will do
It has dressed itself in frost
It is more immediate
than any image of my making.

You say it's not a poem
It is a blade of grass and grass
is not quite good enough
I offer you a blade of grass.

You are indignant
You say it is too easy to offer grass
It is absurd
Anyone can offer a blade of grass.

You ask for a poem
And so I wrote you a tragedy about
how a blade of grass becomes more and more difficult to offer

And about how as you grow older
a blade of grass becomes more difficult to accept.

Brian Patten

Talk about

- How do the writers use different techniques to create a similar sense of atmosphere?

- How do the poems sound when you read them aloud? Does it bring out any differences between them?

- How do the writers make the audience feel their poems are very personal?

Closer reading

Word and sentence work

In the sonnet...

1 List as many words as you can that describe how the writer feels.

2 This poem contains a lot of **opposites** or **antitheses**, e.g. 'peace' and 'war' in the first line. Highlight, in different colours, or list each pair you can find.

3 Because the poem uses antithesis, each line is in two parts. Highlight the place where you think each break occurs. Why do you think the poem uses this unusual structure? What effect does it have on the poem? You may need to read the poem several times before you come up with an answer.

4 Highlight or list sets of rhyming words. Do these words have anything in common? Why do you think the poet has chosen to link them together in this way?

In *A Blade of Grass*...

5 This is a very repetitive poem, with grass mentioned nine times. Underline any other examples of repetition you can find. Look at the words in the poem and its other features. Why do you think Patten chose to write it like this?

6 'It has dressed itself in frost'. Why has the writer chosen this particular image to describe the grass? What impression is he trying to create? Write down three other ways of saying 'It is covered in frost'. Which do you think is most effective? Why?

Text and genre work

7 Why does Brian Patten want to give his partner a blade of grass? Why is she reluctant to accept it?

8 What makes the ending of this poem so sad?

9 Comparing texts. Make yourself a chart so you can compare these poems. Use the plan below to help you.

	Sonnet	A Blade of Grass
Language		repetitive
Structure	tightly controlled	
Imagery		
Subject		
Atmosphere/ feelings		slow, sad, regretful
Effect		

Writing practice: write your own sonnet

A sonnet is a very tightly structured form of poetry and this can make it hard to write. Here Wyatt makes it easier by repeating the same kind of ideas again and again, always using opposites to get his point across.

- Think of opposites and put them together. You will probably start off with very obvious ideas, e.g. 'running' and 'stopping', 'shouting' and 'whispering' and so on, but the more you think about it, the more unusual and interesting they will become.

- List as many of these as you can. You can put them into a poem when you have worked out how to fit them together. A simple way of doing this is to use the same phrase at the beginning of each line, e.g. 'You remind me of…' or 'Loving you is like…'

Wyatt's poem is written in lines that are ten syllables long, which helps give the poem a regular rhythm.

- Structure your own lines in the same way. You may have to change words, cut some out, or add some to make it work.

- Think about how this changes the sound of what you have written.

- Next, try pairing up some of the ideas in possible rhymes. You may have to change the last word or the word order to make it work. Leave out any that don't work.

- Now fit the different lines together. A sonnet is 14 lines long. You can choose a rhyme scheme to suit yourself, if you prefer not to use the same pattern as Wyatt.

- Read it through. If it sounds good, it's finished!

Follow up!

Get together with other members of your class to make a booklet of the sonnets you have written.

Classbook reference
Unit 21, pages 243–4

There are two passages in this unit. The first is an extract from Charles Dickens' *Oliver Twist*, the story of a young boy growing up in the nineteenth century. His life is hard and he often meets with great cruelty. One of the characters who has an influence on his life is Fagin, who runs a pickpocketing gang, and tries to get Oliver to join them. This scene is taken from near the end of the book. Oliver has finally been rescued but Fagin has been arrested and is to be hanged for his crimes the next day.

The second is a letter to *The Times*, written by Charles Dickens after he had witnessed a hanging.

Oliver Twist

'Is the young gentleman to come too, sir?' said the man whose duty it was to conduct them. 'It's not a sight for children, sir.'

'It is not indeed, my friend,' rejoined Mr Brownlow; 'but my business with this man is intimately connected with him; and as this child has seen him in the full career of his success and villainy, I think it well – even at the cost of some pain and fear – that he should see him now.'

These few words had been said apart, so as to be inaudible to Oliver. The man touched his hat; and glancing at Oliver with some curiosity, opened another gate, opposite to that by which they had entered, and led them on, through dark and winding ways, towards the cells.

'This,' said the man, stopping in a gloomy passage where a couple of workmen were making some preparations in profound silence – 'this is the place he passes through. If you step this way, you can see the door he goes out at'.

He led them into a stone kitchen, fitted with coppers for dressing the prison food, and pointed to a door. There was an open grating above it, through which came the sound of men's voices, mingled with the noise of hammering and the throwing down of boards. They were putting up the scaffold.

From this place they passed through several strong gates, opened by other turnkeys from the inner side; and, having entered an open yard, ascended a flight of narrow steps, and came into a passage with a row of strong doors on the left hand. Motioning them to remain where they were, the turnkey knocked at one of these with his bunch of keys. The two attendants, after a little whispering, came out into the passage, stretching themselves as if glad of a temporary relief, and motioned the visitors to follow the jailer into the cell. They did so.

The condemned criminal was seated on his bed, rocking himself from side to side, with a countenance more like that of a snared beast than the face of a man. His mind was evidently wandering to his old life, for he continued to mutter, without appearing conscious of their presence otherwise than as a part of his vision.

'Good boy, Charley – well done –' he mumbled – 'Oliver, too, ha! ha! ha! Oliver, too – quite the gentleman now – quite the – take that boy away to bed!'

The jailer took the disengaged hand of Oliver, and whispering him not to be alarmed, looked on without speaking.

'Take him away to bed!' cried the Jew. 'Do you hear me, some of you? He has been the – the – somehow the cause of all this. It's worth the money to bring him up to it – Bolter's throat, Bill; never mind the girl – Bolter's throat, as deep as you can cut. Saw his head off!'

'Fagin,' said the jailer.

'That's me!' cried the Jew, falling instantly into the attitude of listening he had assumed upon his trial. 'An old man, my lord; a very old, old man!'

'Here,' said the turnkey, laying his hand upon his breast to keep him down – 'here's somebody wants to see you – to ask you some questions, I suppose. Fagin, Fagin! Are you a man?'

'I shan't be one long,' replied the Jew, looking up with a face retaining no human expression but rage and terror. 'Strike them all dead! What right have they to butcher me?'

As he spoke he caught sight of Oliver and Mr Brownlow. Shrinking to the farthest corner of the seat, he demanded to know what they wanted there.

'Steady,' said the turnkey, still holding him down. 'Now, sir, tell him what you want – quick, if you please, for he grows worse as the time gets on.'

'You have some papers,' said Mr Brownlow, advancing, 'which were placed in your hands for better security by a man called Monks.'

'tis all a lie together,' replied the Jew. 'I haven't one – not one.'

'For the love of God,' said Mr Brownlow solemnly, 'do not say that now, upon the very verge of death, but tell me where they are. You know that Sikes is dead, that Monks has confessed, that there is no hope of any further gain. Where are those papers?'

'Oliver,' cried the Jew, beckoning to him. 'Here, here! Let me whisper to you.'

'I am not afraid,' said Oliver in a low voice, as he relinquished Mr Brownlow's hand.

'The papers,' said the Jew, drawing him towards him, 'are in a canvas bag, in a hole a little way up the chimney in the top front room. I want to talk to you, my dear; I want to talk to you.'

'Yes, yes,' returned Oliver. 'Let us say a prayer. Do! Let me say one prayer – say only one, upon your knees with me, and we will talk till morning.'

'Outside, outside,' replied the Jew, pushing the boy before him towards the door, and looking vacantly over his head. 'Say I've gone to sleep – they'll believe you. You can get me out if you take me so. Now then, now then!'

'Oh! God forgive this wretched man!' cried the boy, with a burst of tears.

'That's right, that's right,' said the Jew; 'that'll help us on. This door first if I shake and tremble as we pass the gallows, don't you mind, but hurry on. Now, now, now!'

'Have you nothing else to ask him, sir?' inquired the turnkey.

'No other question,' replied Mr Brownlow. 'I hoped we could recall him to a sense of his position –'

'Nothing will do that, sir,' replied the man, shaking his head. 'You had better leave him.'

The door of the cell opened, and the attendants returned.

'Press on, press on,' cried the Jew. 'Softly, but not so slow. Faster, faster!'

The men laid hands upon him, and disengaging Oliver from his grasp, held him back. He struggled with the power of desperation for an instant and then sent up cry upon cry that penetrated even those massive walls, and rang in their ears until they reached the open yard.

It was some time before they left the prison. Oliver nearly swooned after this frightful scene, and was so weak that for an hour or more he had not strength to walk.

Day was dawning when they again emerged. A great multitude had already assembled; the windows were filled with people, smoking and playing cards to beguile the time; the crowd were pushing, quarrelling and joking. Everything told of life and animation but one dark cluster of objects in the very centre of all – the black stage, the cross-beam, the rope, and all the hideous apparatus of death.

Sir,

I was a witness of the public execution at Horsemonger Lane this morning. I believe that a sight so inconceivably awful as the wickedness and levity of the immense crowd could be imagined by no man, and could be presented in no heathen land under the sun. The horrors of the gibbet and of the crime which brought the wretched murderers to it faded in my mind before the atrocious bearing, looks, and language of the assembled spectators. When I came upon the scene at midnight, the shrillness of the cries and howls that were raised from time to time, denoting that they came from a concourse of boys and girls already assembled in the best places, made my blood run cold. As the night went on, screeching, and laughing, and yelling in strong chorus, were added to these. When the day dawned, thieves, low women, ruffians and vagabonds of every kind, flocked on to the ground, with every variety of offensive and foul behaviour. Fightings, faintings, whistlings, imitations of Punch, brutal jokes, tumultuous demonstrations of indecent delight when swooning women were dragged out of the crowd by the police, with their dresses disordered, gave a new zest to the general entertainment. When the sun rose brightly as it did – it gilded thousands upon thousands of upturned faces, so inexpressibly odious in their brutal mirth or callousness, that a man had cause to feel ashamed of the shape he wore, and to shrink from himself, as fashioned in the image of the Devil. When the two miserable creatures who attracted all this ghastly sight about them were turned quivering in the air, there was no more emotion, no more pity, no more thought that two immortal souls had gone to judgement, no more restraint in any of the previous obscenities, than if the name of Christ had never been heard in this world, and there were no belief among men but that they perished like the beasts.

I do not believe that any community can prosper where such a scene of horror and demoralisation as was enacted this morning outside Horsemonger Lane Gaol is presented at the very doors of good citizens, and is passed by, unknown or forgotten. And I would ask your readers to consider whether it is not a time to think of this moral evil of public execution, and to root it out.

Talk about

- What are the differences in language between these extracts and more modern texts?

- How does Dickens feel about hanging?

- What are your own reactions when you read each extract?

Closer reading

Word and sentence work

In *Oliver Twist*...

1 Dickens creates a strong sense of atmosphere in the first few paragraphs. Highlight the phrases which create this effect, such as 'gloomy passage'.

2 Look at the descriptions of Oliver and Fagin and the way they speak. What impression is created of each? Pick out five key words or phrases connected with each character and explain why each is important.

3 How does Oliver feel about Fagin? How does Fagin feel about him? Pick out specific evidence from the extract to support your answer.

In the letter...

4 Highlight any words you are unsure of, such as **tumultuous** or **odious**, and find out what they mean. Remember that a dictionary may give more than one definition. Pick out the one that fits best here.

- Write a **glossary** – a list of words and their meanings to accompany the passage – to make it easier for other pupils your age to understand.

5 This passage contains a lot of **emotive language** – words and phrases designed to make the reader react in a particular way. 'The horrors of the gibbet', for example, sounds a lot worse than 'The hanging'.

- Highlight all the examples of emotive language you can find. Rewrite the words under three headings – those that refer to sights, sounds and to Dickens' own feelings. There may be some that fit more than one category.

Text and genre work

6 In the letter, although Dickens claims to be a witness at a hanging, he doesn't describe the event itself. What does he concentrate on instead?

7 In *Oliver Twist*, what are the main reasons Oliver and Mr Brownlow go to see Fagin?

8 In the letter, what effect is achieved by having two paragraphs, a long one followed by a short one?

9 From the evidence in both extracts, what do you think Dickens' attitude to hanging is?

10 Both passages contain descriptions of a crowd preparing to watch a hanging. In what ways are these passages different?

- The extract from *Oliver Twist* has portraits of individual characters; the letter describes the crowd in general. Why do you think Dickens chose to write in this way?

11 Which piece of writing do you think is most effective? Why?

Writing practice: a letter of protest

Write a letter of protest about something you have seen.

- Describe it in detail, and include your reasons for objecting. You can choose something you have seen at first hand, or something you have seen on television. It could be something topical, e.g. hunting, or something more unusual, such as the amount of money wasted at Christmas.

- Think carefully about how to structure your letter.

- Aim to write about five paragraphs:

- **the first:** describe in detail exactly what you are protesting about

- **the next two:** give different reasons for your protest. The more carefully you explain them, the more effective your protest will be

- **the fourth:** explain what will happen if nothing is done about it

- **the fifth:** your conclusion, a round-up of all your main arguments.

Follow up!

See how many different protest letters you can find, in newspapers, magazines and on the Internet. Which are the most effective and why?

Classbook reference
Unit 18,
pages 204–7

A touch of class

In this episode of the TV sit-com, *Fawlty Towers*, Basil has advertised his hotel in an exclusive magazine, hoping to attract a better class of customer – the kind of person he thinks he ought to be mixing with. He is delighted when Lord Melbury checks in – until he finds out the truth about his guest.

BASIL	Your lordship, may I offer you a little aperitif… as our guest?
MELBURY	That's very kind of you… dry sherry if you please. (*he wanders off*)
BASIL	(*to the Major*)… What else?… Such… oh, I don't know what…
THE MAJOR	Je ne sais quoi?
BASIL	Exactly! Exactly! (*Sybil enters*) Ah, there you are, Sybil. *(he departs lord-wards with the sherry)*
SYBIL	Good evening, Major.
THE MAJOR	Evening, Mrs Fawlty. *Melbury is glancing at some coins in a display case. Basil brings him his drink.*
BASIL	There you are, your lordship.
MELBURY	Ah, thank you very much.
BASIL	I see my little collection of coins tickles your interest.
MELBURY	What? Oh, yes, yes.
BASIL	All British Empire, of course. Used to be quite a hobby of mine… little investment too…
MELBURY	Quite… *Meanwhile Polly runs out of the hotel front door and signals to Danny, who is sitting in a car; he flashes his lights in acknowledgement. Back in the bar…*
MELBURY	… Oh yes, you know, these sorts of things, the value's soared this last couple of years.
BASIL	Have they really?
MELBURY	Yes, yes. You take my advice. Get them revalued, and insure them for the full amount.
BASIL	Yes, yes, I will.
MELBURY	Can't take any risks nowadays, I'm afraid.
BASIL	No, no, quite.

MELBURY	Well, I must be off.
BASIL	Thank you, thank you, your lordship. I'll certainly…
MELBURY	*(leaving)* Goodbye.
SYBIL	Basil!
BASIL	Yes, yes, I was just talking to Lord Melbury, dear…
MR WAREING	A gin and orange, a lemon squash, and a scotch and water, please!
BASIL	I do apologise, I was just talking to Lord…
MELBURY	*(coming back in)* Fawlty!
BASIL	*(leaving the Wareings in mid-sentence)* Yes, Lord Melbury?
MELBURY	I was just thinking… I'm having dinner tonight with the Duke of Buckleigh… do you know him?
BASIL	Not… personally, no.
MELBURY	Oh… well, he's a great expert, you know, Sotheby's and all that…
BASIL	Is he?
MELBURY	Well, if you liked, I could take them with me, ask him to have a quick look at them and find out their current value.
BASIL	*(overwhelmed)* Would… would you really?
MELBURY	Yes, yes, certainly. Well, I'll be off in a few moments. *(he leaves)*
BASIL	Well, that's really… so incredibly…
SYBIL	Basil!!
BASIL	I'm talking to Lord Melbury!
MR WAREING	*(slow and loud)* A… gin… and orange… a lemon squash… and a scotch and water, please!
BASIL	All right! All right!
	The reception bell rings urgently; it's Polly. Basil runs out clutching the coins in a box.
POLLY	Oh, Mr Fawlty…
BASIL	Was that Lord Melbury? Has he gone?
POLLY	I rang… Mr Fawlty, I must speak with you.
BASIL	What?… can't you see I'm busy?
POLLY	Please! It's very important – can we talk in there? *(indicating the office)*

BASIL	I can't!
SYBIL	*(calling from the bar)* Basil!!
POLLY	It's very important!
BASIL	*(shouting)* I'm just dealing with something important out here, Sybil, thank you. *(to Polly)* All right! *(they both go into the office)* Yes? Yes, right, well, yes, yes, what is it?
POLLY	It's about Lord Melbury.
BASIL	Yes?
POLLY	He's not Lord Melbury… he's a confidence trickster.
BASIL	… I beg your pardon?
POLLY	Mr Brown told me.
BASIL	*(contemptuously)* Haaa!
POLLY	Mr Brown's from the CID. They've been watching Melbury because he's pulling some big con trick in the town. They're going to arrest him when he leaves the hotel so as not to cause you embarrassment. But he asked me to tell you…
BASIL	*(not believing a word of it)* Oh, how nice of him!
POLLY	Please, Mr Fawlty.
BASIL	Oh, I don't know what other tales Mr Brown of M15 has been impressing you with but…
POLLY	He's a con man!
BASIL	Oh, of course. It stands out a mile, doesn't it. He's so **common** – unlike that cockney git whose ulterior motive will soon no doubt become apparent to you, poor innocent misguided child that you are.
SYBIL	*(entering briskly)* Basil, what is going on?
BASIL	Nothing, my dear, nothing at all.
POLLY	Mrs Fawlty…
BASIL	Now look!
SYBIL	Yes, Polly?
BASIL	I don't know what she's…
SYBIL	Basil!!!

POLLY	Mr Brown's from the CID.
BASIL	Hah!
POLLY	He showed me his identification. They're watching Melbury. He's a confidence trickster.
SYBIL	I see. *(she goes straight to the safe)*
BASIL	What… what do you mean, you see?
SYBIL	Let's have a look at these valuables.
BASIL	What are you doing, Sybil?… Sybil, I forbid you to open the safe! *(she opens the safe)* Sybil, I forbid you to take that case out! *(she takes the case out)* Sybil, do not open that case! I forbid it! *(sits down in dismay; she opens the case)* I never thought I would live to see the day when a peer of the realm… entrusts to us… a case of valuables… in trust.
	Sybil places the open case in front of him. He looks into it for a long time. Then he lifts out an ordinary house brick. Disbelievingly, he shakes it close to his ear, lifts out another and sniffs it, then clinks them together. He puts them down and emits a strange growl.
SYBIL	I'll call the police.

POLLY	They're here already, Mr Brown's outside. *(she leaves; the reception bell rings)*
SYBIL	Someone at reception, Basil.
	Basil rises slowly and goes into reception. Hoping it is Melbury, he has clenched his fist – but it is Sir Richard and Lady Morris.
BASIL	Ah! … all right… *(collects himself)* Good evening.
SIR RICHARD	I believe you were expecting us.
BASIL	No, I was expecting somebody else. *(goes into another reverie)*
SIR RICHARD	Sir Richard and Lady Morris.
BASIL	*(absently)* Yes, yes, them as well.
SIR RICHARD	I'm sorry?
BASIL	How did you know?
SIR RICHARD	What?
BASIL	Oh… you're Sir Richard and Lady Morris, I do beg your pardon. I was just think… er… *(He goes off again, thinking revenge; he comes to)* Now, would you mind filling this out, please, we've given you room… *(Lord Melbury comes down the stairs)* Ah hah!
MELBURY	Ah, Fawlty!
BASIL	Mr Fawlty to you, Lord Melbury.
MELBURY	I beg your pardon?
BASIL	Oh, nothing, please, forget all about it.
MELBURY	Oh… well… here's the cheque for two hundred pounds…
BASIL	Ah, thank you so much.*(he bites the cheque and throws it away; the Morrises are transfixed)* Now, about my priceless collection of coins…

Talk about

● Where in the extract is what we see more important than what we hear?

● In what ways are each of the characters different?

● Which parts did you find funny and which parts do not work?

Closer reading

Word and sentence work

1 Basil addresses Melbury as **Lord Melbury**, whilst Melbury simply calls him **Fawlty**. Polly calls Basil **Mr Fawlty** and he calls her **Polly**. What does this tell us about the relationships between the characters?

2 There are many occasions in the extract when Basil is polite.

● Highlight those places where you think he is being sarcastic, those where he is simply being courteous and those where he is being over-polite.

● What effect does this have on the drama?

● How does it make the audience react to him?

3 Describe how Basil's attitude to Lord Melbury changes as the scene develops.

4 The stage directions (set in italic type) are an important way for writers to indicate what the audience should actually see. What do each of the

following instructions suggest about the attitude of the characters?

● *He puts them down and emits a strange growl.*

● *The Morrises are transfixed.*

● *He departs lord-wards with the sherry.*

Text and genre work

5 Which of the characters do you feel most sympathy for? Why?

6 How do the writers give the impression that Polly's news is urgent?

7 Much of the comedy here works because of contrasts created between the way Basil speaks to Lord Melbury and the way he speaks to the other characters.

● Write a list of the other contrasts in the passage, in order of importance.

● Why do you think the Morrises are included in the scene?

8 Sybil says very little in this extract, but she is still an important character.

● What do we learn about her, from what she says and the way she speaks? Look at the use of punctuation at the end of each of her speeches.

● Look at how Basil and the others react to her, as well as what she says and does.

● How does she contribute to the humour of the scene?

Writing practice: script writing

Write a continuation of the script as the extracts ends and Basil goes inside to talk to his wife and Polly.

● Will he accept that he was wrong?

● Will Sybil have something to say about what has happened?

Try to maintain the characteristics of the way each character speaks. You might find it useful to look back over the extract and pick out two or three phrases or words that seem typical of each of the main characters. Make sure you use them at least once in your script. Try to imagine them speaking your lines – do they work?

Include stage directions. Remember that although your script will tell the audience what the characters say, what they see will also be very funny. Keep directions short, but make sure they give a clear idea of what is happening on stage.

Follow up!

Watch a variety of TV sit-coms. As you watch, jot down a list of the methods used to make them funny. What do they have in common?

Classbook reference
Unit 11, · pages 107–110

In this unit, you will read a complete short story, *The Cloud Child*, by the South African writer, Stephen Black. The writer tells of his visit to Table Mountain, one of the best-known landmarks in South Africa. The story highlights some of the differences in lifestyle and outlook between those who live in the country and those who live in the city.

I once told a stranger that I had never been on the top of Table Mountain, nor halfway up it, although born and brought up in Cape Town. He looked as though he thought I was not speaking the truth. So some months ago I went up, not on foot, I confess, but still to the top. When the mules were rolling in the sand and bracken I took a stroll round the reservoirs and came across a child who was obviously a European, although as brown as many a Cape boy. He was a shy youngster, with ragged hair on his head, and no boots on his feet; dressed in a pair of old knickers and a woollen shirt. Naturally I was surprised. It seemed an astonishing thing that a bare-headed and bare-footed child should be on the top of Table Mountain at seven years of age, while I had not got up there until well on the way to thirty. But it was still more astonishing to find that the boy had never been down the mountain. He had lived in the clouds all his life.

'I was born over there,' he said, pointing to a house at the end of the reservoir. This was after I had overcome his shyness by letting him see a trout line prepared. Presently I pulled out a speckled beauty of at least twenty ounces, and looked at it with some pride. 'I never catch them,' remarked the boy simply. He looked at me in a rather pitiful way, and I could see a tear gathering in each of his eyes as I pulled the hook from the mouth of the wriggling fish. 'I like to watch the fish in the water,' he went on. 'To see them leap, and twist in the sun.'

I put away the fishing tackle, feeling uncomfortable at the look in the child's eyes. 'What is your name?' I asked. 'Philip,' he answered, 'I am called Phil.' I asked by whom, perhaps stupidly. 'By Mother and Father,' he replied, with an air of surprise. He did not know that there were children without parents.

'Tell me what you do here all day long.' It was incomprehensible to me that life on a mountain top could be anything but dull and dreary. We were away from the water now, and the trout was packed in my basket. Somehow I felt sorry I had caught it.

Phil started talking. He got up in the mornings, he said, and went among the pines that grew to the edge of the water to hear the doves coo. The home of every vink was known to him; they built their nests over the water. The Kaffir vinks were beautiful, and so were the suikervogels and swartkops. Then to the valley where the daisies grew, both red and blue. And clumps of everlastings stood higher than his head. There were skulpad and taaibosch to be gathered, but Phil said he never troubled to pick flowers for they grew all around and looked better that way than in a tin fading. In the autumn there was the suikerbosch flower, loaded with syrup, which he collected for his mother to boil down to a delicious kind of treacle. Often he saw buck. They were not very wild, for nobody troubled them with guns or dogs. His dog's name was Mac, and at that time was with his father at the other end of the reservoir.

It was charming to hear this child of the clouds talk. He was so simple and so unhuman. Most town

children of seven are merely inhuman. Phil told me, as we walked to a point from which the town could best be seen, at nights he loved to watch the red spreeuws flying home to the cliffs. They cried out mournfully, and only ate berries; whereas the white-tipped spreeuws sat around his father's cows all day, screamed loudly, and ate the ticks. When we reached the edge of the mountain I cried out with delight at what lay before me. The boy's eyes brightened too. 'I long to go down,' he said, 'do you?'

'I have been down,' I replied, feeling superiority for the first time that day.

'My father has too,' said Phil proudly, 'and my mother says she

went down when I was a little boy. We are all going in the basket on the wire one day.'

The sight was the grandest I had ever seen, but people from abroad tell me to see Table Mountain in the early morning from some miles out at sea is finer. But no impression can efface the one made by the sight from the summit.

Far away were the mountains of Hottentot's Holland. All around peace.

'When I was a little boy,' spoke the child, 'Mother used often to come with me here. She showed me the sea and the ships and the big white houses. But I want to see them close; they are so far away. Does that little ship sail over the sea?' he asked, suddenly pointing to a Castle liner that was steaming out. I told him it did, and that it was not a little ship, but a very big one. Still the ten-thousand-tonner looked small enough from there.

'I see the ships every day,' said the boy. 'They come just as the stars do each night and the flowers in spring; and they go like the birds to their nests. But why do they come and go? It must be a great trouble. And where do the stars go every night? I see them come as I go to bed; but when I get up in the morning they are gone.'

I had a good pair of glasses with me and took them out of my pocket. Phil should have a treat. He shall see the ships and the large white houses. But before I could speak, he said, 'It must be very beautiful down there.

Can you always see the mountain? We often have big, wet clouds around us and then I can't see the ships or the houses. The clouds come over us, and the wind blows. Then Mother says I must stay in the house. What are those little things like daisies on the ground beside the sea?'

Below us on the white sands I could see that a crowd was gathered. 'Those are people,' I said.

'Oh,' he said.

The cloud child asked me many things. I told him of the trains which kept running backwards and forwards beneath pale clouds of smoke, and he was quiet for a long time. 'I want to see a train,' he said at length. 'But I love the big things that run round the mountain and the sea. Father says they are trams pulled by electricity. I don't know what electricity is, but the big trams are fine. They run up the mountain in the dark like moving stars. Mother says they run late at night, but I go to bed before that and see only two trams with stars. When I was a little boy I first saw them, and I thought they were stars that came with the night like the others. They went so fast, as the stars do when they travel. I am going to be very happy when I go down; I shall see all the things I love.'

'I hope so, Phil.'

Then eagerly he went on. 'I see lots of pretty little houses that move about. They go a little and stop a little. I know them all. Every night when I go to bed I think of the little houses on wheels, and say to myself, "Dear God, give me one when I grow up, for Christ's sake. Amen!" Look, look,' he cried suddenly, 'there is one now.'

I took out my glasses and while adjusting them saw a huge vehicle apparently drawn by four horses; but could not make out what it was, for the distance was too great.

'What is it, what is it? My house, my house that goes up and down! Oh tell me!'

I had a suspicion, but did not utter it. Instead, I took a long look through the glasses, and saw a municipal dirt cart. But I did not tell the boy.

Talk about

- What features tell you the story is set in South Africa? Give at least five examples.

- How does the writer concentrate so much into relatively few words?

- How does the writer use description and dialogue to establish the two characters?

- Why is the structure of a story – the way it is put together – important? How is it used to create particular effects here? What are they?

Closer reading

Word and sentence work

1 Pick out three descriptive sentences or phrases. For each, explain why you consider it a vital part of the story.

2 'He was so simple and so **unhuman**. Most town children of seven are merely **inhuman**.' What, in your opinion, is the difference between **unhuman** and **inhuman**? Give examples of these two different kinds of behaviour.

3 The opening of any story is important and gives the reader vital information. Look carefully at the first three sentences.

- What are the key words or phrases in each sentence?

- What impression does the writer create of himself?

- Why does he bother to tell us that not only has he never been **up** the mountain but has never even been **halfway up** it?

- What finally makes him take the trip?

Text and genre work

4 Which of the characters in the story did you like most? Why?

5 The origin of the title of the story is obvious, but the author could have easily chosen several others. Why do you think he chose this one?

6 Throughout the story, one of the features we notice is the difference between the adult narrator and the child. Make a list of all the differences you can find. Next to each, write a short quote from the story which proves your point.

7 At the beginning of the story the narrator thinks he is superior to the child. Why?

- How has his opinion changed by the time we get to the end?
- What is it that changes his mind?

8 Our first impression of the child is that he lives in poverty. As we get to know him, however, we find there is a great deal in his life that is worthwhile. How does the writer give us an impression of this rich experience?

9 The structure of the story – the way it is put together – is important.

- Divide the extract into four sections. You will need to decide where you think the story changes. You might choose your divisions according to changes in setting, mood or in the characters.

- Give each of your sections a title.
- Explain why you have chosen these places to divide the story.

Writing practice: short stories

Write your own short story, using some of the skills you have observed in this one.

Many stories, like this one, are about a journey or a visit which in some way changes the main character: because the experience is unexpected, because they meet someone with a different view of life, or because it makes them reconsider their own point of view. Make this the theme of your own story.

This story is quite short, about 1,500 words. Your own might be shorter, but make sure it is no longer.

Choose your characters, limiting yourself to no more than two.

- You might want to write in the first person, as though you are telling the story, but the character doesn't have to be you.
- Decide who the characters will be. It might be a good idea to choose two contrasting people.
- Think about what they look like, but more importantly, decide what kind of people you want them to be – bad tempered? Selfish? Aggressive?
- Which character will change? How?

The story is to be about a journey. Where to? It needs to be a place you know well enough to describe well, so this can help bring the story to life. The description of the setting can be very important in establishing the right mood for your story. It may provide the opening paragraphs. Remember, however, that just because you know the place well, it doesn't mean your characters will.

Decide on the main events of your story. Something must happen to change the way one of the characters thinks.

If you are still stuck, try **one** of these openings:

- 'John brushed the long greasy hair from his face and stared at the deeply lined face in the mirror. Today of all days.'

- 'The foam-flecked waves…'

- 'I'll never forget the day we set off. We didn't know it then, but it was a journey which would change all our lives.'

Follow up!

Short stories are not just short novels. They have their own special characteristics. Read three or four of your own choice, perhaps from _The Penguin Book of South African Short Stories_. Make a list of the stories you have read and the differences between them.

Classbook reference
Unit 7,
pages 57–60

The writers in these poems are concerned about how it feels to grow old, although they both have a completely different attitude towards their situation. As each looks in the mirror, they have time to think about how they feel.

The Face in the Mirror

Grey haunted eyes, absent mindedly glaring
From wide, uneven orbits; one brow drooping
Somewhat over the eye
Because of a missile fragment still inhering,
Skin deep, as a foolish record of old-world
fighting.

Crookedly broken nose – low tackling caused it;
Cheeks, furrowed; coarse grey hair, flying
frenetic;
Forehead, wrinkled and high;
Jowls, prominent; ears, large; jaw, pugilistic;
Teeth, few; lips, full and ruddy; mouth ascetic.

I pause, with razor poised, scowling derision
At the mirrored man whose beard needs my
attention,
And once more ask him why
He still stands ready, with a boy's presumption,
To court the queen in her high silk pavilion.

Robert Graves

I Look into My Glass

I look into my glass,
And view my wasting skin,
And say, 'Would God it came to pass
My heart had shrunk as thin!'

For then, I, undistrest
By hearts grown cold to me,
Could lonely wait my endless rest
With equanimity.

But time to make me grieve,
Part steals, lets part abide;
And shakes this fragile frame at eve
With throbbings of noontide.

Thomas Hardy

Talk about

● How are the mood and tone of each poem different?

● Which one is intended to be taken most seriously?

● Which features suggest when each one may have been written?

● Which of the poems did you prefer? Why?

Closer reading

Word and sentence work

1 *The Face in the Mirror* contains words that might be unfamiliar to you. Look up the following words in a dictionary to make it easier to follow the main points in the poem. Remember, dictionaries often contain more than one definition. Pick the one that seems to fit best.

inhering	**furrowed**	**frenetic**
jowls	**pugilistic**	**ascetic**
derision	**presumption**	

Graves could easily have chosen a less complicated vocabulary. Why do you think he chose these particular words?

2 *I Look into My Glass* contains fewer challenging individual words, but there are difficult phrases. What does Hardy mean by each of the following expressions?

● 'Would God it came to pass'

● 'By hearts grown cold to me'

● 'lonely wait my endless rest'

● 'lets part abide'

● 'shakes this fragile frame'

Text and genre work

3 In *I Look into My Glass*, what is it about growing old that seems to bother Hardy the most? Is Graves worried about the same things? Which poem seems to you to have the most serious approach to the subject? Choose from the following list of words to describe the tone or mood of each poem:

despairing	**optimistic**
cynical	**obsessed**
self-critical	**thoughtful**
proud	**sensitive**
sensible	**sentimental**
realistic	**warm-hearted**
reckless	**modest**
self-indulgent	**calm**

List your chosen words next to the poems themselves, so you can link them to the parts of the texts that suggest this word to you. You should be able to explain your choice in each case.

4 In earlier questions, you looked at differences in language. Now think about some of the differences in structure. Remember that every feature of a poem has been carefully chosen to create a particular effect on the reader, so when you have spotted a difference, try to explain why it is important. Use the following questions to guide your answers. Bear in mind that all these factors affect the rhythm of the poems.

● Which poem uses a regular rhyme scheme? What effect does this have on the poem as you read it? Which is easier to read? Which is easier to understand?

● Which poem uses lines that are the same length? Does this make it easier or harder to read and understand?

● Which poem uses the most complex sentence structure? How many complete sentences are there in each poem? Which uses the most commas? Which has the largest number of subordinate clauses? Which poem flows more easily as you read it?

5 Using imagery is a way of adding a lot of ideas and feelings to a poem without using a lot of words. 'But time to make me grieve', for example, is a personification, making it sound as though time is alive, with a mind of its own. Using this image, Hardy can suggest:

● he has no control over it

● time is a cruel and heartless enemy

● it is much more powerful than he is.

Stripping back the layers of meaning in an image like this is one of the ways in which you can show your understanding of a piece of literature. Try to suggest similar layers for each of the following images. Remember, there is not necessarily a right answer. It is **your** ideas that count.

'Glaring from wide, uneven orbits'

'Cheeks, furrowed'

'Would God it came to pass
My heart had shrunk as thin!'

'lonely wait my endless rest'

'shakes this fragile frame at eve
With throbbings of noontide'

Writing practice:
an anthology of poems

Growing old is a common subject for poets and writers. Put together your own anthology of poems on the subject, with brief notes for each poem you find, giving guidance about it for a reader of your own age. Make it into a book, with a title and short introduction.

- Finding poems will be easy enough in a library with a reasonable poetry section. You may find what you need by scanning the contents page, since titles often give a good idea of the subject, but you might find flicking through the pages helpful too.

- The Internet also contains libraries of suitable literature which can be easily searched using a key word.

- Various compilations of literature are available on CD-ROM. These can also be easily searched. Ask in your local or school library.

- Try to pick a variety of poems on the subject, positive and negative, old and new. Pick poems that appeal to you. You don't necessarily have to understand every line.

- When you have selected your poems, write an introduction to the book, explaining the reasons for your choice. Pick out any features in the poems you think are worth special comment.

Follow up!

Pick two or three poems from your anthology. With a partner, find a way of reading them aloud that will bring out their most important and interesting qualities. Perform them to the rest of your class.

Classbook reference
Unit 19,
pages 217–19
(similes, metaphors and personification)

She Stoops to Conquer by Oliver Goldsmith is a comedy published in 1773. This is the first scene of the play, where three of the main characters are introduced. The style and structure may be unfamiliar to you, so read it through more than once. You might find it helpful to read it aloud.

Scene – a chamber in an old-fashioned house

Enter Mrs Hardcastle and Mr Hardcastle

Mrs Hardcastle I vow, Mr Hardcastle, you're very particular. Is there a creature in the whole country but ourselves, that does not take a trip to town now and then, to rub off the rust a little? There's the two Miss Hoggs, and our neighbour Mrs Grigsby, go to take a month's polishing every winter.

Hardcastle Ay, and bring back vanity and affectation to last them the whole year. I wonder why London cannot keep its own fools at home! In my time, the follies of the town crept slowly among us, but now they travel faster than a stage-coach. Its fopperies come down, not only as inside passengers, but in the very basket.

Mrs Hardcastle Ay, **your** times were fine times indeed; you have been telling us of **them** for many a long year. Here we live in an old rumbling mansion, that looks for all the world like an inn, but that we never see company. Our best visitors are old Mrs Oddfish, the curate's wife, and little Cripplegate, the lame dancing-master: and all our entertainment your old stories of Prince Eugene and the Duke of Marlborough. I hate such old-fashioned trumpery.

Hardcastle And I love it. I love everything that's old: old friends, old times, old manners, old books, old wine; and I believe, Dorothy *(taking her hand)*, you'll own I have been pretty fond of an old wife.

Mrs Hardcastle Lord, Mr Hardcastle, you're for ever at your Dorothy's and your old wife's. You may be a Darby, but I'll be no Joan, I

---

promise you. I'm not so old as you'd make me, by more than one good year. Add twenty to twenty, and make money of that.

Hardcastle Let me see; twenty added to twenty, makes just fifty and seven.

Mrs Hardcastle It's false, Mr Hardcastle: I was but twenty when I was brought to bed of Tony, that I had by Mr Lumpkin, my first husband; and he's not come to years of discretion yet.

Hardcastle Nor ever will, I dare answer for him. Ay, you have taught him finely.

Mrs Hardcastle No matter, Tony Lumpkin has a good fortune. My son is not to live by his learning. I don't think a boy wants much learning to spend fifteen hundred a year.

Hardcastle Learning, quotha! a mere composition of tricks and mischief.

Mrs Hardcastle Humour, my dear; nothing but humour. Come, Mr Hardcastle, you must allow the boy a little humour.

Hardcastle I'd sooner allow him a horse-pond. If burning the footmen's shoes, frightening the maids, and worrying the kittens be humour, he has it. It was but yesterday he fastened my wig to the back of my chair, and when I went to make a bow, I popt my bald head in Mrs Frizzle's face.

Mrs Hardcastle And am I to blame? The poor boy was always too sickly to do any good. A school would be his death. When he comes to be a little stronger, who knows what a year or two's Latin may do for him?

Hardcastle Latin for him! A cat and fiddle. No, no, the alehouse and the stable are the only schools he'll ever go to.

Mrs Hardcastle Well, we must not snub the boy now, for I believe we shan't have him long among us. Anybody that looks in his face may see he's consumptive.

Hardcastle Ay, if growing fat be one of the symptoms.

Mrs Hardcastle He coughs sometimes.

Hardcastle Yes, when his liquor goes the wrong way.

Mrs Hardcastle I'm actually afraid of his lungs.

Hardcastle And truly so am I; for he sometimes whoops like a
speaking trumpet – *(Tony hallooing in behind the scenes)* –
O there he goes – a very consumptive figure.

Enter Tony, crossing the stage

Mrs Hardcastle Tony, where are you going, my charmer? Won't you
give Papa and me a little of your company?

Tony I'm in haste, Mother; I cannot stay.

Mrs Hardcastle You shan't venture out this raw evening, my dear;
you look most shockingly.

Tony I can't stay, I tell you. The Three Pigeons expects me down
every moment. There's some fun going forward.

Hardcastle Ay; the alehouse, the old place: I thought so.

Mrs Hardcastle A low, paltry set of fellows.

Tony Not so low neither. There's Dick Muggins the exciseman, Jack Slang the horse-doctor, Little Aminadab that grinds the music box and Tom Twist that spins the pewter platter.

Mrs Hardcastle Pray, my dear, disappoint them for one night at least.

Tony As for disappointing **them**, I should not so much mind; but I can't abide disappointing **myself**.

Mrs Hardcastle *(detaining him)* You shan't go.

Tony I will, I tell you.

Mrs Hardcastle I say you shan't.

Tony We'll see which is the strongest, you or I!

(Exit, hauling her out)

Talk about

- What features make plays different from novels?

- What evidence is there that the play was written in the eighteenth century?

- Which lines, ideas or characters do you find amusing?

- Which characters do you find attractive?

Closer reading

Word and sentence work

1 Many of the names of the characters are unrealistic – **Tony Lumpkin, Mrs Oddfish, Cripplegate**, for example.

- What impression do these names give of the characters?

- **Mr Hardcastle** is a more normal name – why do you think the writer chose it, when the others are so strange?

- What can we guess about the character of a man with such a name?

2 You may find some words in the passage unfamiliar.

- Highlight **affectation, follies, fopperies, trumpery, haste, exciseman,** and any others you think are important. Find out what they mean. Remember, a dictionary may give more than one definition. Pick the one you think is most suitable. **Consumptive,** for example, is defined as '**tending to consume or tending to be affected with consumption**'. Consumption has several definitions, and you will need to think about the rest of Mr and Mrs Hardcastle's discussion, to come to the conclusion that it is a '**wasting disease**'.

- The play's vocabulary is one of the things that identifies it as an eighteenth-century work, but the way phrases are constructed is also important. 'I was but twenty', for example, could easily be modernised by replacing **but** with **only**. All that has changed is the way we use the word **but**.

Pick out five other short phrases in the extract that need only small changes to make them easier for a modern audience to understand. For each one, explain what has changed – is it the way a word is used, the order the words are placed in, or is it a word we don't use any more?

3 The characters of Mr and Mrs Hardcastle are clearly intended to be very different. Divide your page into two columns, one for each character, and write down what we find out about:

- their attitude to Tony
- their opinion of 'a trip to town'
- what they think of old age.

Text and genre work

4 The three characters feel very differently about each other. Which of the following words could you use to describe the relationship between:

- Mr and Mrs Hardcastle
- Tony and his mother
- Mr Hardcastle and Tony.

respectful	scornful
selfish	loving
patronising	indulgent
hostile	cruel
honest	domineering
rebellious	suspicious

5 *She Stoops to Conquer* is a comedy. Goldsmith uses several devices to make the audience laugh, including:

- the contrast between Mr and Mrs Hardcastle
- the way Mrs Hardcastle treats her son
- Mrs Hardcastle's vanity
- Mr Hardcastle's remarks about Tony.

Find an example in the text of each of these devices.

Are there other ways in which the passage is made funny? Mark these too, using your own system.

6 What is your opinion of each of the characters?

● Do you think Mr Hardcastle treats his wife fairly?

● Do you think Mrs Hardcastle deserves to be spoken to in the way Tony does?

● Do you think Tony is a lively teenager with a mind of his own, or is he selfish and spoilt?

7 Look back at your work on *Fawlty Towers*. The two passages are similar since they are both drama scripts. Are there any other similarities between them? Look at:

● the way the characters speak

● the use of humour

● the way the characters relate to each other.

Writing practice: directing the play

When you read an extract from a play such as this, it is easy to forget that it is not how you are supposed to experience it. You are supposed to see and hear it. A group of actors performing this piece would be able to use a whole range of devices to get the audience to react the way they want them to.

Write a detailed set of instructions for the three actors playing this scene, so they would know exactly how to present it.

● Start by describing the set. What do you want the room they are in to look like? Rich and elegant? Seedy and threadbare? Do you want a lot of props or just a few?

● How do you want your characters dressed? Although this play is set in

the eighteenth century, you may prefer to use more modern dress – many productions do. This is one of the first things the audience will notice and you could give a wonderful first impression of Mrs Hardcastle by presenting her properly. Remember, she is a very vain woman who thinks of herself as being much younger than she is. You could also highlight some of the differences between Tony and Mr Hardcastle. You could illustrate your ideas by drawing cartoons, exaggerating whatever features of the characters you feel are appropriate.

● How will your characters speak? This will vary as the scene progresses and may change depending on who a character is talking to. What kind of accent do you want them to use? At which points will their voices be soft or loud? Fast or slow? Angry or amused? Sarcastic or pleading?

● What will the actors do? Will they be standing or sitting? How? Will they be close together or apart? You don't need to go through the entire scene explaining every change. Instead, pick out key points where you want something to happen. If, for example, Mr Hardcastle is sitting in a huge leather armchair and Mrs Hardcastle is kneeling in front of him when the scene opens, it will give the impression that he is very much in control. Is that what you want? If Mr Hardcastle crosses the room and turns his back when Tony comes in, it tells you a lot about their relationship.

● Remember, every decision you make will have an effect on the way the audience see – and interpret – the play. Try to explain the effect you are trying to create and why you think it is important. You might find it helpful to draw brief sketches to help your explanations.

Follow up!

Conflict between parents and children is not unusual. Think about TV programmes you have seen in which this subject is raised. What appear to be the most common reasons for family fall-outs in these dramas? Do they have anything in common with the Hardcastles' problems?

Classbook reference
Unit 16, pages 172–6

Making history: the truth about Henry VIII

The extracts you are going to read here are all about Henry VIII. The first is part of an entry in *Encarta,* a CD-ROM encyclopedia. The second is taken from *The Terrible Tudors* in the *Horrible History* series, designed to interest young readers in some of the less obvious facts about life in the past. The third is from Neville Williams' book, *Henry VIII and his Court,* a glossy biography containing large numbers of photographs as well as detailing the events of the King's life.

Extract 1

Henry VIII (1491–1547), Tudor King of England (1509–1547), and founder of the Church of England. The son of Henry VII, he profoundly influenced the character of the English monarchy.

Henry was born in London on June 28, 1491, and on the death of his father in 1509, succeeded to the throne (his elder brother Arthur having died in 1502). He then married his brother's widow, Catherine of Aragon, having been betrothed to her through a papal dispensation secured in 1503. This was the first of Henry's six marriages, which were affected by the political and religious conditions of the time and by the monarch's increasingly despotic behaviour. At the beginning of his reign, Henry's good looks and hearty personality, his fondness for sport and the hunt, and his military prowess endeared him to his subjects. A monarch of the Renaissance, he entertained numerous scholars and artists, including the German painter Hans Holbein the Younger, who painted several portraits of the King and members of his court.

A question of divorce

In 1511 Henry joined in the Holy League against France, and in 1513 he led the English forces through a victorious campaign in northern France. Meanwhile, France's ally, James IV of Scotland, led an invasion of northern England which was crushed in September 1513 at Flodden Field by Henry's commander, Thomas Howard, 2nd Duke of Norfolk, with the death of the King and many Scottish nobles. Deserted by his allies, Henry arranged a marriage in 1514 between his sister Mary and Louis XII of France, with whom he formed an alliance. Louis's successor, Francis I, met Henry at a magnificently staged meeting on the Field of the Cloth of Gold in 1520, but no significant political decisions resulted.

Extract 2

- Henry is famous for his six wives. But, did you know that in just one year (1536) his first wife (Catherine) died, his second (Anne Boleyn) was beheaded and he married his third (Jane Seymour).

- Henry was fond of cock-fighting so he had his own cock-fighting pit built at Whitehall in London. There are different battles fought on the site today – it is number 10 Downing Street, the home of the Prime Minister!

- Henry was famous for his love of music. He composed many pieces and was a keen singer. He owned ten trombones, 14 trumpets, five bagpipes, 76 recorders and 78 flutes. It is said he composed the tune, *Greensleeves*.

- Henry was a show-off. He organised a great tournament near Calais in France, known as the **Field of the Cloth of Gold**. It seemed mainly a chance for him to display his own sporting talents. He is said to have tired out six horses while performing a thousand jumps … **to the delight of everyone**.

- Henry fancied himself as a wrestler. At a wrestling contest at the **Field of the Cloth of Gold** he created a stir by challenging King Francis I of France with the words… **'Brother, we will wrestle'**. Francis couldn't refuse even though Henry was taller and heavier. Francis used a French-style trip and won – the English thought this was cheating; the French probably thought it served big Henry right.

- Henry liked to play an indoor tennis game called 'Paume'. He didn't go to see his wife, Anne Boleyn, executed. He was playing tennis while she had her head chopped off. As soon as he was brought the news of Anne's death, he rushed off to see his next love, Jane Seymour.

- Even hard Henry VIII had a heart. He needed a son to carry on the Tudor royal name. He was so furious when Anne Boleyn produced baby Elizabeth that he refused to go to the christening!

- Henry wanted to get rid of Anne Boleyn for giving him only a female child. Her other babies died. One of the things he accused her of was being a witch. He had some support from the Tudor people in this. Anne had been born with a sign of the devil on her… she had six fingers on her left hand!

- Only his third wife, Jane Seymour, gave him the son he wanted – then she died a few days later. Of his six wives, it was Jane Seymour he asked to be buried next to when he died.

Extract 3

Exceptionally tall and well-proportioned, the young Henry naturally commanded the stage with an easy authority. Looks and stature were not everything in a King, but to tower over all others helped. Short, stocky sovereigns, ugly even, and indifferently dressed, as Louis XI of France had been, could dominate their courts, but a King who had the figure and features of a Greek god and moved

gracefully was in an enviable position. The most ignorant of subjects could easily identify him as he rode by. Keeping himself trim with exercise, there was as yet no suspicion of surplus weight, no hint that this handsome youth would swell into a grotesque, gross Goliath. A foreigner thought him 'the handsomest potentate I have ever set eyes

on … with an extremely fine calf to his leg'. Indeed, his youth gave Henry an unfair advantage over the Emperor Maximilian, with his snub nose and huge jaw, over Ferdinand I of Aragon, whose shifty looks did not belie his nature, and over the old *roué* Louis XII of France, riddled by syphilis. Henry was clean shaven, had a very fair complexion and his auburn hair, 'combed short and straight in the French fashion', set off a rounded face with the features so delicately formed that they 'would become a pretty woman', though his throat and neck were 'rather long and thick'.

Outside England both his character and appearance were unknown; yet a single meeting was enough to give a lasting impression of his personality and potential. 'Hitherto small mention has been made of King Henry, whereas for the future the whole world will talk of him,' predicted a Venetian in London. England, it was soon apparent, was ruled by a colossus who could not be ignored. That shrewd political commentator, Niccolò Machiavelli, who never met Henry, described him by repute as 'rich, ferocious and greedy for glory'.

England was to have a queen again, who with her own train of attendants, would enliven the palace and smooth some of the roughness of manners at court. Since the death of Elizabeth of York in 1503, Henry VII had put out diplomatic feelers for a successor and even made tentative proposals for the hand of the mad Joanna of Castille, but he had remained a widower.

The new King announced he would in fact marry Catherine of Aragon, to fulfil his father's death-bed wish – the same princess who had been brought from Spain as the bride of his elder brother, the ill-starred Arthur. Since Arthur's death she had lived, almost incarcerated, in Durham House, on a meagre allowance amidst quarrelsome servants and intriguing confessors, wondering if she would ever marry Henry, to whom she had been betrothed since his twelfth birthday.

Henry and Catherine were married very quietly six weeks later in the chapel of the Franciscan Observants at Greenwich, to enable the coronation on Midsummer Day to be a double crowning of King and Queen. The coronation was scarcely over when the death of the old Countess of Richmond, Henry VIII's grandmother, and the pillar of English humanist studies, snapped another link with the past.

Talk about

- What are the differences and similarities between each of the passages?

- What kind of people might read each one?

- Why has each writer selected the information they have used?

Closer reading

Word and sentence work

1 Complete the table below, by adding examples in the appropriate places, to help you identify some of the differences in the language used in the three passages.

	Encarta	*The Terrible Tudors*	*Henry VIII*
Verbs			riddled
Adjectives			
Nouns	prowess		
Abbreviations		couldn't	
Connectives			yet

2 Which passage makes most use of **emotive language**? (i.e. words and phrases designed to make you react in a particular way, such as 'Henry was a show-off'. We react against this because we don't normally like people who show off).

Text and genre work

3 Look at the third passage. Highlight those parts which you consider to be **opinions** rather than **facts**. Remember, a fact is something that can be proved.

4 In the third passage, what is the writer's opinion of Henry? You will need to look at particular words and phrases to help you decide – for example, 'a colossus who could not be ignored' and 'features of a Greek god'. Pick out other phrases which support your view.

5 Suggest a title for each of the three passages. Explain why you think each one is suitable.

6 The second passage is aimed at a much younger audience than the other two. How do the writers try to interest their readers? You will need to look at:

● the conversational tone of the extract

● the language used

● how the information is presented.

You might find it helpful to compare each of these features with the other two passages, before you begin to write.

7 Identify all the **facts** (things that can be proved), in all three passages. Why do you think these facts in particular have been used by all three writers? Are other facts included that you think are

important to an understanding of Henry's reign? Which passage contains the most? Why do you think this is the case?

8 Which of the passages do you find easiest to read? Which is the hardest? Which is the most interesting? Which contains the most useful information? If you'd been asked to research Henry's life, which extract would you find most helpful?

9 Imagine you have been asked to publish new editions of all three books. You have been asked to suggest an illustration for each one. What would you suggest? Write a description, or draw a sketch for each one. You can choose cartoons, photographs, paintings or any other artwork you think suitable. Explain why you have chosen each one.

Writing practice: writing to inform

You are going to write an information sheet for primary school children to help them do a project about Henry VIII. You will need to think about:

● **facts:** which facts will you include from each of the three passages? Which will younger children find most interesting? Which do they need to know in order to produce a balanced project?

● **language:** the language you use will be important. You will not be able to copy anything from the original passages – don't forget those writers have a completely different aim from you. You need to remember who your audience is as you choose each word and sentence, so you can be sure they will understand it. Think about the length of sentences and paragraphs. More importantly, you need to think about how you will draw the pupils into Henry VIII's life, so they will be interested and want to find out more for themselves. Remember, you are not just selecting facts – you are writing your own sheet. Choosing suitable adjectives and constructing your own emotive phrases will help make your work individual and original.

- **presentation:** this will also be important. Will you write in columns? Will you divide your work into sections? How will you use titles and sub-headings to make it look attractive and easy to read?

- **illustrations:** use illustrations if you think this will improve your finished information sheet.

- **imagination:** be imaginative! Your finished product should be informative, but most of all it should look and sound interesting.

Follow up!

Gather together as much information as you can about the present-day royal family. Look in books, newspapers, on television, the Internet and in magazines. Try to decide how much of the information you gather is factual and how much is someone's opinion. You might try writing your own *Horrible History*-style entry, using the material you've found.

Classbook reference
Unit 12, pages 118–20

For hundreds of years, travellers have felt the urge to share their experiences with others. In the thirteenth century, Marco Polo travelled a great deal in the Middle and Far East. Most people in Western Europe knew little about these areas and were fascinated by his tales, which were a mixture of personal observations, history and stories he had heard. Sometimes it is not easy to tell the difference between them, as you will see from the three extracts below. Henry Fielding, the novelist, seems more interested in the people he met on his voyage to Lisbon in 1754.

The Travels of Marco Polo

Extract 1

The above-mentioned khalif, who is understood to have amassed greater treasures than had ever been possessed by any other sovereign, perished miserably under the following circumstances. At the period when the Tartar princes began to extend their dominion, there were amongst them four brothers, of whom the eldest, named Mangu, reigned in the royal seat of the family. Having subdued the country of Cathay, and other districts in that quarter, they were not satisfied, but coveting further territory, they conceived the idea of universal empire, and proposed that they should divide the world amongst them. With this object in view, it was agreed that one of them should proceed to the east, that another should make conquests in the south, and that the other two should direct their operations against the remaining quarters. The southern portion fell to the lot of Ulau, who assembled a vast army, and having subdued the provinces through which his route lay, proceeded in the year 1255 to the attack of this city of Baldach. Being aware, however, of its great strength and the prodigious number of its inhabitants, he trusted rather to stratagem than to force for its reduction, and in order to deceive the enemy with regard to the number of his troops, which consisted of a hundred thousand horse- besides foot-soldiers, he posted one division of his army on the one side, another division on the other side of the approach to the city, in such a manner as to be concealed by a wood, and placing himself at the head of the third, advanced boldly to within a short distance of the gate. The khalif made light of a force apparently so inconsiderable, and confident in the efficacy of the usual Mahometan ejaculation, thought of nothing less than its entire destruction, and for that purpose marched out of the city with his guards; but as soon as Ulau perceived his approach, he feigned to retreat before him, until by this means he had drawn him beyond the wood where the other divisions were posted. By the closing of these from both sides, the army of the khalif was

surrounded and broken, himself was made prisoner, and the city surrendered to the conqueror. Upon entering it, Ulau discovered, to his great astonishment, a tower filled with gold. He called the khalif before him, and after reproaching him with his avarice, that prevented him from employing his treasures in the formation of an army for the defence of his capital against the powerful invasion with which it had long been threatened, gave orders for his being shut up in this same tower, without sustenance; and there, in the midst of his wealth, he soon finished a miserable existence.

Extract 2

In the middle of the hall, where the Grand Khan sits at table, there is a magnificent piece of furniture, made in the form of a square coffer, each side of which is three paces in length, exquisitely carved in figures of animals, and gilt. It is hollow within, for the purpose of receiving a capacious vase, shaped like a jar, and of precious materials, calculated to hold about a ton, and filled with wine. On each of its sides stands a smaller vessel, containing about a hogshead, one of which is filled with mare's milk, another with that of the camel, and so of the others, according to the kinds of beverage in use. Within this buffet are also the cups or flagons belonging to His Majesty, for serving the liquors. Some of them are of beautiful gilt plate. Their size is such that, when filled with wine or other liquor, the quantity would be sufficient for eight or ten men. Before every two persons who have seats at the tables, one of these flagons is placed, together with a kind of ladle, in the form of a cup with a handle, also of plate; used not only for taking the wine out of the flagon, but for it to the head. This is observed as well with respect to the women as the men. The quantity and richness of the plate belonging to His Majesty is quite incredible.

Extract 3

Here are seen huge serpents, ten paces in length, and ten spans the girt of the body. At the fore part, near the head, they have short legs, having three claws like those of a tiger, with eyes larger than a fourpenny loaf and very glaring. Jaws are wide enough to swallow a man, the teeth are large and sharp and their whole appearance is so formidable that neither man, nor any kind of animal, can approach them without terror. Others are met with of a smaller size, being eight, six, or five paces long; and the following method is used for taking them. In the daytime, by reason of the great heat, they lurk in caverns, from whence, at night, they issue to seek their food, and whatever beast they meet with and lay hold of, whether tiger, wolf or any other, they devour; which they drag themselves towards some lake, spring of water, river, in order to drink. By their motion in this way along the shore and their vast weight, they make a deep impression, as if a heavy beam had been drawn along the sands. Those whose employment is to hunt them observe the track by which they are most frequently accustomed to go, and fix into the ground several pieces of wood armed with sharp iron spikes, which they cover with the sand in such a manner as not to be perceptible. When therefore the animals make their way towards the places they usually haunt, they are wounded by these instruments, and speedily killed.

A Journal of a Voyage to Lisbon

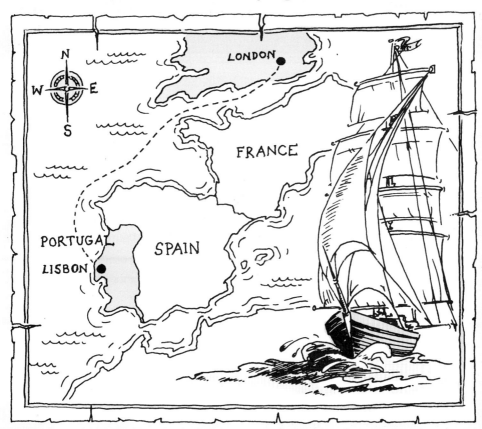

Mrs Francis.

She was a short, squat woman; her head was closely joined to her shoulders, where it was fixed somewhat awry; every feature of her countenance was sharp and pointed; her face was furrowed with the smallpox; and her complexion, which seemed to be able to turn milk to curds, not a little resembled in colour such milk as had already undergone that operation. She appeared, indeed, to have many symptoms of a deep jaundice in her look; but the strength and firmness of her voice overbalanced them all; the tone of this was a sharp treble at a distance, for I seldom heard it on the same floor, but was usually waked with it in the morning, and entertained with it almost continually through the whole day.

Though vocal be usually put in opposition to instrumental music, I question whether this might not be thought to partake of the nature of both; for she played on two instruments, which she seemed to keep for no other use from morning till night; these were two maids, or rather scolding-stocks, who, I suppose, by some means or other, earned their board, and she gave them their lodging gratis, or for no other service than to keep her lungs in constant exercise.

She differed, as I have said, in every

particular from her husband; but very remarkably in this, that as it was impossible to displease him, so it was as impossible to please her; and as no art could remove a smile from his countenance, so could no art carry it into hers. If her bills were remonstrated against she was offended with the tacit censure of her fair-dealing; if they were not, she seemed to regard it as a tacit sarcasm on her folly, which might have set down larger prices with the same success. On this latter hint she did indeed improve, for she daily raised some of her articles. A pennyworth of fire was to-day rated at a shilling, to-morrow at eighteenpence; and if she dressed us two dishes for two shillings on the Saturday, we paid half a crown for the cookery of one on the Sunday; and, whenever she was paid, she never left the room without lamenting the small amount of her bill, saying: 'she knew not how it was that others got their money by gentlefolks, but for her part she had not the art of it'. When she was asked why she complained, when she was paid all she demanded, she answered: 'she could not deny that, nor did she know she had omitted anything; but that it was but a poor bill for gentlefolks to pay'.

Talk about

- Which words and phrases are unfamiliar to you?

- What have these extracts got in common? What makes them different?

- Which parts did you find amusing, unrealistic or interesting?

- Which extract did you prefer to read? Why?

Closer reading

Word and sentence work

In *The Travels of Marco Polo...*

1 One of the things that makes this piece of writing quite difficult to follow is the unfamiliar combinations of words.

For example, in the first extract, 'Upon entering it...' In more modern text, this would probably be replaced by 'When he went in'. Write a modern equivalent of each of the following phrases:

- 'the khalif made light of a force apparently so inconsiderable'

- 'he feigned to retreat before him'

- 'he soon finished a miserable existence'.

2 In the second extract, Marco Polo is impressed by the richness of the scene. List the words and phrases he uses which describe this sense of wealth.

In the third extract, Marco Polo describes terrible 'serpents'. How does he try to give an impression of how dangerous they are?

3 What is the writer's opinion of Ulau, in the first extract? What do each of the following phrases suggest?

● 'He trusted rather to stratagem than to force'

● 'advanced boldly'

● 'after reproaching him with his avarice'

In *A Journal of a Voyage to Lisbon…*

4 The description of Mrs Francis is critical of her, but is not intended to be taken too seriously. Highlight those parts of the text where Fielding suggests:

● she is very greedy

● she shouts a lot

● she is very ugly.

5 Using a different coloured pen, highlight those parts of the extract where you think Fielding must be exaggerating (using hyperbole).

6 The second paragraph is particularly difficult to follow. What does Fielding mean when he says 'she played on two instruments' and 'these were two maids, or rather scolding-stocks'?

Text and genre work

In *The Travels of Marco Polo…*

7 How does Ulau defeat the khalif of Baldach?

8 Which of these extracts seems to you the most unrealistic? Explain why.

Do you think the original, thirteenth-century audience would have felt the same? Why?

Comparing texts

9 Which of these two examples of travel writing seems to you of most interest to the modern reader? Why? Do they have anything in common with more modern examples you have read (from the Key Stage 3 Classbook, for example)? What do you think is the purpose of this kind of writing? Does it offer anything more than a collection of personal impressions?

Writing practice: a stranger's view

The three extracts from Marco Polo describe a story he has heard, something he has seen, and the local wildlife. Choose **one** of these options and write a passage about a place you have visited or the area you live in. The intended audience is people who have never seen the things you are describing, so aim to impress them, just as Marco Polo intended to astonish readers with his reports of what he had seen and heard.

Remember, things that seem very familiar to you will be completely outside the reader's experience. Describing something as simple as a cat hunting a sparrow could seem dangerous, exciting or unpleasant, depending on how you describe it.

The structure of your writing is important. You must avoid a list, so make sure you plan what you will write about in each paragraph. Using the example above, for example, you could write three paragraphs:

- **paragraph 1:** might describe the cat itself. You could use images to create the effect you are seeking – 'It has fur as soft as…'

- **paragraph 2:** could describe the cat stalking its prey, using emotive language such as 'terrible claws'

- **paragraph 3:** might describe how the chase ends. You could include some details about your own feelings.

Follow up!

Collect photographs which show something of your own travels. Put them in order. Write about them.

Classbook reference
Unit 20, pages 229–31